THE LAST HEDGEHOG

Pam Ayres

THE LAST HEDGEHOG

Illustrated by Alice Tait

PICADOR

First published 2018 by Picador
an imprint of Pan Macmillan
20 New Wharf Road, London N1 9RR
Associated companies throughout the world
www.panmacmillan.com

ISBN 978-1-5098-8126-0

For Arthur, Charlotte, Hugo and Rose

Introduction

I was brought up in rural Berkshire but as a child saw surprisingly few hedgehogs. It was only when I started work that I really began to think about them. My daily route took me past Hatford Warren, a large local wood, where every morning the road was littered with dead hedgehogs, run over in the night. It was awful to see. I remember wishing that people could be warned to slow down on that particular bit of road, but nothing was ever done.

The next time I remember seeing a hedgehog close up, was after I married and had two little children. There was a gate in our garden and for some reason a loop of string hung down from the bottom bar, almost touching the path. One morning I found a hedgehog dead in the loop of string. It had walked into it like a noose and remained there until it died. Its little waving feet had worn bare patches on the ground below. It was heartbreaking. If only I had noticed the string, cut it off, taken it away.

When I first heard about wildlife rescue centres I was ecstatic. *Finally* there was somewhere to take a wounded animal where people would care. I met Les Stocker MBE, the great pioneer who went on to found Tiggywinkles, the first ever hospital for wild animals in 1983. His back garden was filled with cage upon cage of needy hedgehogs. Unlike me, who only stood around wishing things were different, Les had actually gone out and *done* something.

I heard about my own local wildlife rescue centre, Oak & Furrows, founded by the wonderful Serena Stevens in memory of her daughter Millie. I became a supporter, then a patron, and there I saw the hundreds of hedgehogs brought in every year. I know that hardly anybody *means* to harm hedgehogs. Like me, with the deadly noose of string left hanging from my gate, often we just don't think. In this little book I am asking if you will bear them in mind. Please, if you don't already, *think hedgehog*.

Hedgehogs are easy to help. A little food left out at night and some water during hot dry periods mean the stark difference between life and death. A simple pile of logs and clippings in a quiet corner makes a comfortable home. So many of these things are small in themselves but combine to be a help of mighty proportions to our dwindling population of hedgehogs.

My little poem deals with their plight, and all of the fates I describe in it are met with on a regular basis. You are allowed to laugh at it, but the message is serious. This book highlights many easy ways to help hedgehogs recover from their disastrous decline, so that perhaps they could return to their traditional place in our gardens and hedgerows.

Cousin Henry, young and bright,
Went up in flames on Bonfire Night

And poor old grandpa, fast asleep,
Was stabbed to death in a compost heap.

My uncle in one playful bound
Fell in a swimming pool and drowned,

My aunt was old, her eyes had dimmed,
But all the same she wound up strimmed.
You didn't look, you didn't see,
And there she goes. An amputee.

If in your fence you'd made a space

We could have moved from place to place,

Have found a gal, paid our respects,
Had some cautious hedgehog sex,

And in a cosy pile of logs
Produced a nest of little hogs.

From now on, as you pull the drapes
You'll see no round familiar shapes,
Nevermore from dusk till dawn
Will we eat slugs on your lawn,

So little gratitude you've shown
From now on you can eat your own.

Drowned in rubbish, drowned in junk,
That's why our population's shrunk,
You threw down stuff you couldn't use,

The plastic rings from packs of booze,
Polluted, poisoned, burned and mowed,
And ran us over on the road.

If you'd been a hedgehog's friend,
You'd give your pond a shallow end,

And so, farewell, for what it's worth
From the final hedgehog left on earth,
In garden netting tightly wound
I have no hope of being found.

Some curtain call. Some final bow.
You crocodiles.

                  Start crying now.

Tips to make your garden more hedgehog friendly

- Make sure your garden has a 5in (13cm) square gap in boundary fences or walls. They travel about a mile each night so need access to plenty of gardens!

- Keep a corner of your garden wild to offer shelter, protection and natural food.

- Avoid using pesticides and slug pellets in your garden. These can harm hedgehogs and damage their food chain.

- Provide a shallow dish of fresh water and food such as meat-based pet food for hedgehogs, especially during long dry spells.

- Check areas thoroughly for hedgehogs and other wildlife before strimming or mowing.

- Dispose of litter responsibly. It can cause injury or starvation if they get trapped in discarded rubbish.

- Bonfires offer a tempting home for a hedgehog, collected materials should be re-sited just before the fire is to be lit and the pile should be checked very carefully for wildlife or pets in need of rescue before lighting.

BRITISH HEDGEHOG PRESERVATION SOCIETY

Hedgehog House, Dhustone, Ludlow, Shropshire SY8 3PL

Tel: 01584 890 801

www.britishhedgehogs.org.uk

@hedgehogsociety

/hedgehogsociety

Take a look at the online shop selling all kinds of
hedgehoggy goodies!